Horses of the Sea

Carol Hosking

Contents

Introduction

What is a fish but looks like a horse?

What has a pouch like a kangaroo but doesn't hop?

What has a long tail like a monkey but doesn't swing from the trees?

It's a seahorse!

It's easy to see how the seahorse got its name. It really does look like a horse. However, this amazing creature is actually a small fish, found bobbing in shallow seas throughout the world.

A herd of horses

There are 32 different kinds of seahorse in the world. The seahorse also has many relatives such as seadragons, pipefish, shrimpfish, and trumpetfish.

Although they look very different, they all have three things in common:

- long, tube-shaped **snouts** with jaws that don't move

- **armour**-coated bodies and fast-moving fins

- the ability to use **camouflage**.

Seadragon

Shrimpfish

Pipefish

Seahorses come in many shapes and sizes. Some are as small as one centimetre; most do not grow longer than about 35 centimetres.

Trumpetfish

An underwater stable

Seahorses and their relatives live in oceans all around the world, except for the **polar** areas. They swim in the shallow waters along coastlines, around **coral reefs**, and among seaweed.

Longsnout seahorses swim in shallow waters around North and South America.

The speckled seahorse is a visitor to the south-western shores of the United Kingdom.

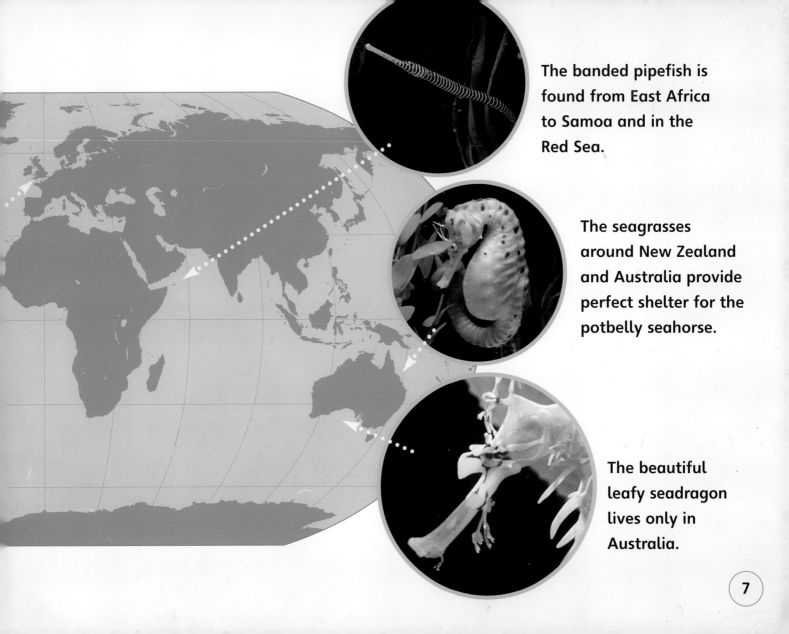

The banded pipefish is found from East Africa to Samoa and in the Red Sea.

The seagrasses around New Zealand and Australia provide perfect shelter for the potbelly seahorse.

The beautiful leafy seadragon lives only in Australia.

Tougher than they look

A seahorse may appear to be delicate, but this unusual creature is tougher than it looks. With no teeth or scales, the seahorse depends on its unique armour-plated body to protect it from enemies. This 'coat of armour' is made up of ring-like, bony **plates** dotted with **spines**. While these hard rings protect the seahorse, they make its body rather stiff.

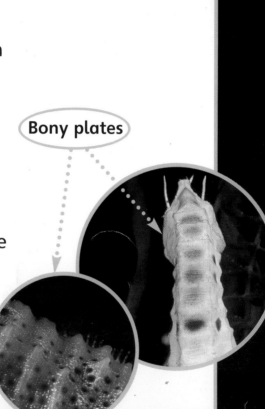

Bony plates

The stiff body of the seahorse prevents it from swimming like other fish. Instead, the seahorse is forced to bob up and down or glide forward in long spurts. It fans its back fin faster than the eye can see.

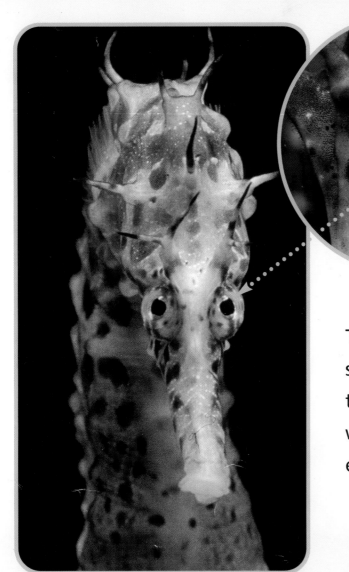

The seahorse's eyes move in separate directions. This allows the seahorse to look for food with one eye and check for enemies with the other.

Finding food

Seahorses eat only live food such as shrimp and other small **crustaceans**. All seahorses and their relatives have stiff jaws, and most have no teeth. They suck in their food with their 'vacuum cleaner' mouths and swallow it whole.

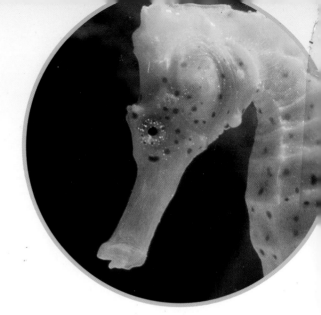

A seahorse sucks in its prey.

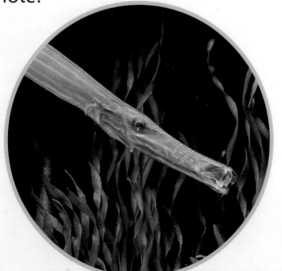

The Pacific trumpetfish does have some teeth, but still sucks in its food.

Although seahorses are fish, they have some special features that make them different from other fish.

Similarities	Differences
• fins • gills • backbone • cold-blooded	• armour plates instead of scales • toothless, vacuum-like mouth • independently moving eyes • moves by bobbing or gliding because body is rigid

Weird things about seahorses

Seahorses are fascinating, but they are a bit weird! Seahorses begin each day by dancing together. A male seahorse curls his long tail around a blade of grass to anchor himself and stays very close to home. His **territory** may be only one metre wide. Meanwhile, the female may swim ten times as far, searching for food and producing eggs. However, she will always return to dance with her mate in the morning.

Home is where you tie up your tail and stay for a while.

The seahorses' daily dance lasts six to ten minutes.

The most unusual thing of all about seahorses is that the father gives birth to the young. There are very few animals whose males do this.

The female gives the male hundreds of eggs to carry in his pouch. When the babies are ready to be born, they are pushed out into the wide, watery world through a small opening in the pouch. They must learn to look after themselves immediately.

Baby seahorses
leave their
father's pouch.

Although lots of animals change shape or colour to avoid enemies, seahorses are among nature's best at hiding themselves.

Some **species** of seahorse look very much like the grasses where they make their home. Other brightly coloured species blend easily in to the colourful coral reefs where they live.

Seahorses and seadragons can grow leafy-looking skin that resembles the plants and coral they live in.

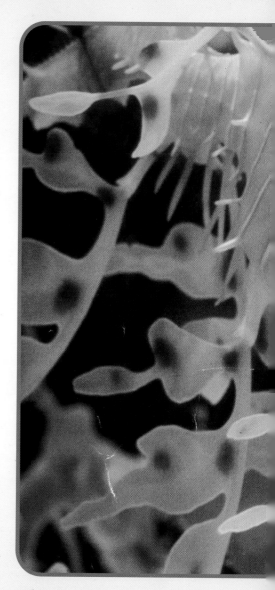

This leafy seadragon blends right in to his seaweed home.

Long, thin alligator pipefish are hard to spot among seagrasses.

Baby shrimpfish protect themselves by hiding among the spikes of sea urchins.

A race against time

No one knows how many seahorses live in the wild, but we do know from the reports of seahorse fishers that they are able to find only half as many as they did just a few years ago. It is thought that more than 20 million seahorses are caught each year. Most of these end up in medicines that are sold in other countries.

This scientist studies seahorses to help protect them.

About a million seahorses are captured alive each year for **aquariums**. Many of these are bought for home aquariums in countries where seahorses make popular pets. Sadly most owners do not understand how difficult seahorses are to keep. Seahorses must eat live food — and they have big appetites. They also get ill very easily. Most of the seahorses in home aquariums die within a few months.

Saving the seahorse

Many people are now involved in seahorse **conservation**. An international organisation called Project Seahorse was set up in 1996 to help **preserve** seahorses in the wild. The work being done by Project Seahorse includes:

- studying seahorses and their habitats
- educating people who buy or sell seahorses
- setting up conservation programmes in fishing areas

If you want to find out more about Project Seahorse go to **www.projectseahorse.org**, e-mail **info@projectseahorse.org** or write to:

Dr Heather Hall, Zoological Society of London,
Regents Park, London, NW1 4RY

Index

Glossary

aquarium a tank containing fish and other sea animals

armour a hard covering that protects the body

camouflage a way of colouring something so that it is hard to see against the things around it

conservation protecting things from dying out

coral reef an underwater bed of hard, stony sea-creatures

crustacean an animal with a hard shell that lives in water

plate a section of scale or bone

polar near the North or South Pole

preserve to keep alive

snout the long nose of an animal

species a type or family of animals or plants

spine a spiky piece of bone that sticks out

territory an area that is guarded by one animal